More Praise For

CONVERSATION SECRETS FOR TOMORROW'S LEADERS

21 Obvious Secrets Leaders Do Not Use Enough

"If you are looking to transform your organization so everyone feels empowered to do their best, read Conversation Secrets for Tomorrow's Leaders by Dr. Mindy Gewirtz, Steve Hamilton-Clark and Carrie Gallant. The book does a masterful job providing 21 ways leaders can use conversations to build trust, connection, and collaboration. A quick, practical read, this profound book will guide you to change your work culture, and the world, one conversation at a time."

- Dr. Marcia Reynolds, named #5 in the Top Global Coaching Gurus, and #1 female coach, and author of *Coach the Person, Not the Problem* and *The Discomfort Zone: How Leaders Turn Difficult Conversations into Breakthroughs*

"Conversations are essential. Leaders cannot afford to miss out on the conversation secrets that Mindy, Steve and Carrie are sharing. Whether it's building your network, leading your team, implementing strategy or managing stakeholder relationships, mastering these conversation secrets will take you to the next level in your career."

- May Busch, former COO Morgan Stanley Europe, now executive coach, speaker, advisor and author of *Accelerate: Nine Capabilities to Achieve Success at Any Career Stage.*

"If communication is humanity's 'free' superpower this book is an excellent investment to help you become a communication superhero."

- Dan Pontefract, leadership strategist and best-selling author of *Lead. Care. Win, Open to Think* and *The Purpose Effect.*

"Everything meaningful in business and in life happens through conversations. Leaders in all walks of life – lawyers, business owners, parents – need to connect, build trust and inspire collaboration to accomplish the great things we are here to do. Conversation Secrets for Tomorrows' Leaders primes you for the personal growth required to up-level your ability to have and hold the conversations that will move you, your relationships and your work forward in the world."

- Ali Katz Esq., CEO of New Law Business Model, named to Entrepreneur Magazine's 100 Powerful Women of 2020, and author of *The New Law Business Model Revealed: Build a Lucrative Law Practice That You (And Your Clients) Love.*

"Mindy, Steve and Carrie deftly acknowledge the changing times leaders are having to navigate and they do so with respect, understanding and thoughtfulness. In straightforward and practical ways these experienced coaches provide a treasure trove of tools and ideas to help leaders build trust, conversation and collaboration at a time we need it most. This is a must-read for leaders and those aspiring to be one."

- Cinnie Noble LLM, founder of CINERGY® Coaching and author of *Conflict Management Coaching: The CINERGY® Model*

"Despite the global impact of covid-19, there's something to give us hope, a ray of light amid the gloom--for me, it's this book. The authors offer actionable points for leaders to communicate with empathy, building trust, connection and collaboration. Packed with practical advice, this book is a call for hope for leaders, in these and other challenging times."

- Professor Raju Vir, Master Certified Coach (MCC), Senior Leadership Coach for C-Suite and top teams, Senior Leadership Coach at Saudi Telecom (STC), Prism Award Finalist 2019 (ICF)

To Yvette

CONVERSATION
SECRETS
FOR TOMORROW'S LEADERS

21 OBVIOUS SECRETS
LEADERS DO NOT USE ENOUGH

Carrie

DR. MINDY L. GEWIRTZ
STEVE HAMILTON-CLARK
CARRIE E. GALLANT

Cover design and image: Moonlit Fox Design

Print ISBN: 978-1-73646-1-600
eBook ISBN: 978-1-73646-1-617

Printed in the United States of America.

First Edition

TABLE OF CONTENTS

CHAPTER THREE   53
The Language of Collaboration

PREFACE

Why Did We Write This Book?

At the heart of writing this book is our passion—Mindy, Steve, and Carrie's—to prepare tomorrow's leaders for the global awakening happening today. The 21 conversation secrets are perhaps obvious—as often the best secrets are "hidden in plain sight." We chose these 21 secrets from our collective decades-long experience coaching senior leaders around the world. These secrets are easy to learn and require practice to sustain impact. Yet we have witnessed time and again, that leaders forget, avoid, or don't use these conversational tools enough to heighten their leadership impact to truly make a difference. These secrets are conversational tools essential for developing the culture of trust, connection, and collaboration needed for innovation at the best of times, and during volatile and uncertain times.

What is The World Context in Which We Find Ourselves?

The world has changed dramatically since COVID-19 in the year 2020. This Pandemic has unleashed a tsunami of volatility and uncertainty. For the first time in history, we struggle as a world humanity to manage the contagion and its life threatening impact. Global, public, and private partnerships work feverishly to develop and eventually distribute vaccines. Hopefully by the end of 2021 whoever wants to be vaccinated will have had that opportunity. This virus, in the meantime, has crippled the global economy and challenged humanity's collective belief in its invincibility.

Millions of people have died, been hospitalized, or fallen ill. Millions more remain unemployed. Global populations have been mandated by their governments into lockdown in their homes for months at a time. This translates into working from home, and schooling children, teens, and college students at home. Travel and in-person contact are extremely limited, stripping people of social cohesion with family, friends, and within their communities. Many thousands of neighborhood small businesses and large favorite retail icons such as JC Penny, Neiman Marcus, and Lord & Taylor declared bankruptcy and closed their doors.

At the same time, the voices of diverse people who had previously been rendered voiceless are beginning to be heard. Their conversations have been ignored for so long and they're fed up with hollow talk and promises not kept. These people are rising, taking their voices and conversations to the streets resulting in an awakening around the world. They have chosen to make visible their invisibility through protests that confront those who control both policy and the economy. Their request is to be heard, to create greater justice, and to advance a more equitable world where everyone can benefit. Conversations regarding racial injustice, diversity, and political differences are igniting on the streets like dry brush in the scorching sun and threaten to engulf the entire country in an angry conflagration.

The second conversational discourse that provides the context for this book, is the difficulty friends, neighbors, and families have had in discussing opposing political views. The amount of anger and frustration people are experiencing in these exchanges, points to the need for better conversational tools. This is true for leaders in organizations, families, and communities. We need to learn how to speak together productively and listen to diverse points of view and learn from one another.

The third and broader context is how the paradigmatic shifts occurring in biology, economics, and the future of work have accelerated the pace of change. Learning and applying the conversational secrets can exponentially charge the shifts taking place beyond individual leaders to their leadership teams, organizations and global networks.

This unprecedented worldwide sense of vulnerability and ensuing awakening of hope for change that we are experiencing compelled the three of us colleagues—Mindy, Steve, and Carrie—to make a difference by adding value to the conversation about how best to meet these seismic shifts. We realize that it would mean, first and foremost, introducing equally "awakened" modes of communication. As seasoned executive coaches working with C-Suite and tomorrow's leaders, teams, and organizations, we began sharing our coaching secrets on how to help our clients—senior leaders in organizations—have powerful conversations with employees working at home, or with those slowly returning to work during this uncertain time.

Coaching these leaders, we recognized how the prolonged stress of managing individuals, teams, and organizations during this upheaval was taking a toll on them as well. We find in our coaching conversations that leaders are also looking to inspire trust and create meaningful connections with people in a post-trust world. The black swan event of the pandemic and its aftermath requires more than a business pivot used when the market changes or a disaster occurs. The convergence of the global pandemic, the volatile economy, political disruption, and climate unsustainability gives rise on a visceral level that something of great magnitude is occurring. It is as if we are trying to conduct business as usual even as we hear the pounding of hooves of the Four Horsemen that signal the Apocalypse approaching in the distance.

While this doomsday-like scenario is one spin on the events we are seeing, we invite you to consider a more optimistic interpretation.

Our perspective of this "2020 turning" is that we are witness to a positive, lifechanging tipping point for humanity. This pandemic has exponentially accelerated an awakening that until now has only gradually progressed in the 21st century. We believe humanity possesses the gift of free will and has the capacity to choose a new paradigm shift from that of scarcity to abundance, from competition to collaboration, from situations where only the few thrive to that of an evolving capitalism where all people can experience abundance.

How might humanity change, from this point forward? Consider how we might communicate with one another, how we could conduct business and allocate global resources if we choose collaboration over competition. In the corporate world, this has gone by various names such as, "Conscious Capitalism" or "Stakeholder Capitalism." This means that beyond shareholder profits, corporations serve the best interests of all their stakeholders including customers, communities, employees, and even the climate. How we communicate and navigate all these interests is optimized when we co-create a culture of trust, connection, and collaboration.

Communication is humanity's "free" superpower—it is our ability to share in thinking and feeling, to be sentient, to process patterns and make meaning. How we use conversation for good or for bad is our choice. We can create conversations of hate or enmity towards one another – and we have seen that during the pandemic—or we can use our conversations to develop trust, to connect, to develop relationships, and to collaborate in teams or networks to solve complex problems. We have seen this during the pandemic as well, as universities and global pharmaceuticals that sometimes compete have come together to expedite development of a vaccine.

How we communicate has a powerful impact in this post-trust world. Many people have lost trust of elected leaders, of company leaders they work for, and in each other. This is our opportunity to change that.

We invite you to practice these 21 secrets of communication that have the power to obviate the breakdowns and lapses brought about by the pandemic, the economy, and eroding social cohesion. As Simon Sinek said in his September 2017 Ted Talk, "Leadership is not about being in charge. Leadership is about taking care of those in your charge." Leaders who are skillful at applying these communication tools with individuals, teams, and embed them throughout their organizations will succeed in leading people through the challenges of the coming decade with greater positive impact.

These 21 secrets provide leaders the capacity to develop psychological safety, to speak with empathy and to restore trust, connection, and collaboration. When leaders transform themselves first, people follow, and a new culture of trust and collaboration can become the cornerstone for innovation to thrive.

INTRODUCTION

Why Conversation Tools in Three Chapters?

People across the divides of race, gender, and demographics are speaking up to change the world we live in. Yes, conversations have become polarized. We firmly acknowledge, however, that humanity can change and find common ground. But it will take some skill building and conscientiousness to get there. That is where the 21 secrets come in, divided into Three Chapters.

Chapter One focuses on secrets for developing and sustaining Trust, as trust is the bedrock of conversations for leaders who want to effect change. Establishing one's integrity, and clarifying values for example, pave the way for trust in how you lead a team and set the direction for an organization.

Chapter Two is about Connection, and here we discuss how leaders can master the types of conversations that connect people to each other, one team to another within and across the organization, and the organization to the broader network of stakeholders, so that change can flourish.

In Chapter Three we delve into Collaboration. Once individuals experience trust, and a language of connection is established, things start to get exciting as a unique dynamic grows that encourages creativity and innovation. This chapter includes various secrets you can practice within or across your teams and embed collaboration throughout the organization.

Collaborative conversations are built on both the bedrock of trust and the infrastructure of connection. They're the lifeblood pumping throughout the structure of the organizations to create a thriving culture that is adaptive to changes and constantly innovating.

Example: Leaders Creating Stakeholder Capitalism through Conversations

A recent example of leaders creating powerful change through conversations is the development of Stakeholder Capitalism at the World Economic Forum led by Klaus Schwab, founder, and executive chairman of the World Economic Forum. Schwab worried that the project on identifying metrics for companies that embraced this evolved capitalism beyond benefiting shareholders would fade away given the pandemic. Instead, the pandemic accelerated acceptance of the need for corporations to change. The project was completed, and the metrics were ratified and distributed to the public in the fall of 2020.

As Schwab wrote in the Times Magazine Special Report, November 2, 2020: "But in a world where pessimism is increasingly the order of the day, and narrow and short-term self-interest is still alluring, initiatives like these demonstrate that a more inclusive and sustainable model is possible. It is up to us to replicate and follow such an approach."

We invite you to consider that the conversational secrets of trust, connection, and collaboration can become an intrinsic part of the global reset. The cascading impact of individuals, teams and organizations applying the 21 conversation secrets, and the awakening occurring in the world, can lead to more stakeholder-centric organizations embracing Stakeholder Capitalism.

Our intent is to elevate the conversation. These secrets will inspire you to find your own voice and to speak up in new ways. As you learn to embed conversations into the workplace that are inclusive of all employees, your confidence as a leader will grow. Consider these conversation tools also applicable wherever you find yourself in life, as leadership is distributed everywhere—in our own families, in our communities, and wherever people are in a position to plant the seeds for a better world for future generations.

This handbook of conversational secrets is our contribution for leaders, and we are all leaders in our own right, in our way, in our own time. Everyone reading this book has the above-mentioned superpower within, and by practicing these tools you can build the trust, connection, and collaboration to lead humanity into the future, one conversation at a time. We hope you will invite others to practice together with you. As we have found in writing this book, we three have grown from our many conversations and collaborative efforts.

Share with us how you have used these tools and what happened as a result. We look forward to having an ongoing dialogue with you and all our readers.

Mindy Gewirtz

Stephan Hamilton-Clark

Carrie Gallant

CHAPTER ONE

The Language of Trust

You are a good leader. You know it, and so do your people. However, the black swan event of the pandemic, the economic fallout, and the ensuing uncertainty that has taken hold has jolted your reality. This is your leadership crucible. You must adapt and grow, deep and fast, into a great leader in half the time. Otherwise, you and the people in your company will end up staying home for good. You know what to do with the customers, with markets, with products, and with managing capital. That's the easy part. What's of great concern is how to lead when trust is at an all-time low, when people are so disengaged, and the outside world (beyond the pandemic) doesn't feel safe. This is the recurring dream that keeps you up at night. What is a great leader to do?

You start considering your own values and that of the company, and how they calibrate. You make certain to "walk your talk" as you begin to align with your north star and use language which reflects that. You focus on integrity as the currency of trust because people know when a leader is being truthful or when they're delivering the "company line." You are more mindful of how you demonstrate integrity daily with your family and at work. You begin honing your ability to truly listen and to empathize. You convey clarity of purpose and terms of engagement for any new project and are more resilient in the face of new information and opinions.

SECRET 1:
SPEAK WITH INTEGRITY

Be Impeccable with Your Word.
Speak with integrity. Say only what you mean.

Avoid using the word to speak against
yourself or to gossip about others.

Use the power of your word
in the direction of truth and love.

- Don Miguel Ruiz

Successful people and leaders know that when you speak and act with integrity, not only do you feel intrinsically good and right with yourself, but other people who also respect and trust you, are more likely to want to be in relationship with you and do business with you.

In a recent study of 195 leaders in 15 countries over 30 global organizations, 67% chose "has high ethical and moral standards" as the #1 competency for the question: "What makes an effective leader?"

Perhaps this is why so many companies have "Integrity" in their corporate values list.

"Integrity" tops the list of common values of Fortune 500 companies, and is frequently expressed as an over-arching personal value, such as in James Clear's annual "Integrity Reports."

And yet.

Without supporting actions, integrity is just a word. There is something ineffable about integrity. We know it when we see it. And when we don't, we sense that too. It's like a sniff test. Blatant lack of integrity can assault the senses, while subtle lacks in integrity can give a feeling of something just not being right.

Warren Buffett refers to integrity as one of three qualities to look for when hiring people: Integrity, Intelligence, and Energy. "And if they don't have the first one, the other two will kill you," he concludes.

Indeed.

Witness the contrast between two famous companies that faced disastrous scandal: Enron and Johnson & Johnson. Laughably, one of Enron's corporate values was Integrity. However, its leaders' actions were in direct opposition to that value. As renown business coach and best-selling author, Brian Tracy said, "Enron's success was built on lies, and the 'winners' who headed the company are case studies in lack of integrity."

On the other hand, when Johnson & Johnson faced the poisoned Tylenol deaths scare in 1982 and 1986, it simply acted with integrity, and pulled its product, despite a $100 million loss. J&J leaders spoke and acted with integrity, by assuming responsibility for public safety and re-building public confidence.

As defined by Hall of Fame football coach, Tony Dungy, integrity is "the choice between what's convenient, and what's right."

Speak with integrity. Act with integrity. And perhaps most importantly, take responsibility.

Take responsibility for your words and actions, and their impact. This takes courage, regular self-reflection, and the ability to silence the thousand voices in your head to listen to your one voice of inner wisdom.

Others will follow your lead. Employees will bend over backwards for leaders who have integrity.

SECRET 2:

TAP INTO VALUES FOR GREATER IMPACT

It's not hard to make decisions
when you know what your values are.

- Roy Disney

In his book, *"The Advantage,"* Patrick Lencioni outlines six critical questions every leader, team, and organization must answer. The first question is "Why do we exist?" The second question—which is the focus of this Secret—is, "How do we behave?"

A good part of the answer to "How do we behave?" lies in defining and honoring one's values. When leaders consistently and consciously align their decisions to their values (and those of their team/organization), over time, they're more likely to have a positive impact on others' lives (and their own).

Why? Because people working together learn to appreciate what to expect from each other, and from there emerges relationships of high trust—the key ingredient to accessing the Executive Brain for transformational conversations.

Further, given the increasingly Volatile, Uncertain, Complex, and Ambiguous (VUCA) world in which leaders operate, values-based decision making allows leaders to transcend pre-conditioned belief structures so that they can become more aware of who they are and lead more authentically.[2]

Barack Obama openly led his White House team based on the value of integrity, and together they made decisions that honored this value. Operating in a hostile bi-partisan environment, Barack Obama and his team lived relatively scandal-free during his eight-year term.

Values define what is most important to us; they form the framework we use for making decisions and are the driving force behind our work and our passions. Organizations recognize the power of values. Just look at how they publish, support, and promote their corporate values as a guide on how to interact with others.

Leaders who invest time in defining their Top 5 to 10 values and regularly review how well they're honoring them, make better decisions with greater positive impact. A quick first step to defining values—yours, a colleague's, or even a company's—is to ask where you/they spend their Time, Money, and Energy.

We invite you to open your door towards clarifying your values by taking a few minutes for reflecting on where you spend your Time, Money, and Energy.

SECRET 3:
NAME IT!

*When awareness is brought to an emotion,
power is brought to your life.*

- Tara Meyer Robson

Emotions always come first (it's our energy in motion)—then thinking, and then desired outcomes. When our emotions guide our behavior without sufficient thinking and consideration, we are likely to experience an amygdala hijack (flight, fight, freeze, or appease). The outcomes are rarely productive.

When in conversation with someone, silently naming how we feel is a powerful technique that provides our "thinking brain" time to catch up with our "emotional brain." This technique interjects that ever crucial split second or more that is likely to allow for the next thing that comes out of our mouth to be oriented towards a more productive outcome.

"Name it!" can also be used to seek understanding with someone you're speaking to. By sharing what you see them doing or hear them saying—whether explicitly or implicitly—you create a moment for checking in with them and getting more on their wavelength.

An example of "Name it":

> "Joe, it sounds like the client's demands for overnight delivery
> has really got you rattled. What if we take a minute to think this
> through together?"

Overall, "Name It!" works effectively in getting you and others you're working with to slow down, consider feelings, and to let all concerned make more deliberate decisions with the right combination of thought and emotion for maximum leadership impact.

Importantly, staying unattached to what you named provides your listener (and you) the opportunity to let it go to uncover other emotions at play, or explore it further towards a meaningful outcome.

SECRET 4:
MANAGE EXPECTATIONS

We are gathered here today...

This phrase which opens one of those most memorable of occasions—a wedding—sets clear expectations for what is about to take place. The agreement is made, the vows or promises are declared, and this sets the stage for what is expected in the marriage itself.

Just as with a momentous life event, successful people and leaders know that envisioning and setting clear expectations is critical to achieving what is wanted, especially when working with others. Delineating clear expectations is like making a psychological contract. This is what we call: "ground rules," "rules of engagement," or "team norms."[1]

Clear expectations create a safe and reliable environment where creativity and innovation can flourish and where people feel empowered to act and find solutions to any problems that may arise.

Managing expectations is easier when they're clear, shared, and agreed upon in advance. Anything "out of bounds" can be clearly identified and addressed. Clarifying expectations helps to avoid gaps in understanding or false assumptions that can lead to unnecessary conflict.

Why?

Clarity dispels confusion and uncertainty—two states which trigger the amygdala and fear-based reactions and resistance. When someone is left guessing what is expected of them, their minds fill in the gap with stories based on their experience that might not align with your unstated expectations.

Setting and managing expectations is important when:

- Holding a meeting;

- Starting a new project;

- Entering a new relationship (e.g., business partnership, new employee, new client, marriage, or cohabitation);

- Having an important or difficult conversation (e.g., negotiation, managing conflict), and;

- Mediating an issue, conflict, or dispute.

How does one establish healthy, clear, and shared expectations?

- Be willing to share your intentions and goals.

- Listen to connect.

- Ask questions and seek to understand others.

- Adopt a "we" focus rather than an "I" focus.

Explore, in the spirit of mutual gain, what types of agreements you need to achieve your goals.

SECRET 5:

CHECK IN WITH YOUR MIND'S EYE

My failures have been errors in judgment, not of intent.

- Ulysses S. Grant

We are on the cusp of exponential change. Currencies, the financial world, driverless cars, digitization, real estate, the way our lives are organized, are all going to look different. Do we have the capacity to keep up? We're not built for this kind of exponential change. What we do have is our ability to adapt and grow. Even our brain is changing in order to synchronize with the changes. But, as we adapt to the new way, we must be careful not to be caught in the net and lose that human piece of us. Intentionality is important. We need to use our language to reclaim some of what we lost and are at risk of losing in the future.

How can we begin to accomplish this on an individual level? How can we build up a language of trust and interdependency?

We often enter a conversation with the right intention, but the message doesn't always have the intended impact. In fact, research suggests that 9 out 10 times our messages fail to land effectively![2] Our message gets interpreted by the listener based on their store of life experiences which are used to make sense of what we're saying. Sometimes it's as if we are in the same theatre watching different movies. The same images are projected onto the screen but we each see, hear, and experience the movie differently.

When we focus only on our own agenda, we can come across as being "I-centric" which in turn triggers the listener's primitive brain of "fight, flight, freeze, or appease." Trust levels dial down quickly as a result. Neuroscience tells us that to dial up trust levels, both speaker and listener need to operate from their prefrontal cortex (commonly referred to as The Executive Brain) and become "we-centric." It is in this part of the brain where trust, integrity, empathy, and the capacity for envisioning exist.

To operate from their prefrontal cortex, successful people tap into their mind's eye and literally see themselves in real time hovering above the conversation that is taking place between themselves and the listener. They take note of the impact they're having (call it a "helicopter view" of the conversation) and they check in with themselves and their state of being. Depending what they see and feel, they will seamlessly come back into the conversation and test assumptions about their impact with the listener and read the results.

The speaker does this by creating an environment which invites candid, behavioral feedback. In other words, the speaker articulates what they see/feel/hear is going on. This is typically accomplished through an enquiry. This opens communication and makes the conversation two-way and allows the speaker to test their assumptions about their perceived impact.

An example of enquiry:

> "I may be off-track here, but you don't seem too enthused with the idea. I'm curious. What's on your mind?"

The, "I may be off track here" piece, creates a safe environment for the listener to express themselves, and the "I'm curious" piece acts as an invitation to explore, and naturally brings the listener into their Executive Brain (i.e., the prefrontal cortex) where building trust is most possible.

People who develop the skill to have candid, honest conversations in which a kind of neutral curiosity is at play, set themselves apart, and consistently achieve greater impact.

In your next conversation, test one of your third eye (mind's eye) assumptions and notice the positive impact.

SECRET 6:

ADMIT MISTAKES AND THRIVE

Any fool can defend his mistake—and most fools do.

- Dale Carnegie

Back in 2008, Deborah, the CEO of a consultancy agency, was managing the fallout from the Global Economic Crisis. Determined to make up lost revenue and profit, she made the strategic decision to venture into unknown territory by pitching into a new business sector. Her team subsequently won a large project that involved digital profiling, an area in which she and her team had little expertise.

Despite working 24/7 Deborah's team missed several client delivery deadlines. It quickly became apparent that she and her team were out of their depth.

Deborah had a choice to make on how to move forward: walk away from the project and admit defeat or salvage it somehow. She decided on the latter and called her client counterpart to discuss the situation and explore the way forward. Her client was extremely and understandably upset, and at first, his trust in Deborah's team to deliver was very low. This, however, soon changed. Deborah and her team were able to turn things around for the better.

The key to Deborah's ensuing success was to focus on building trust by creating a meaningful and safe connection with her client. To do so she deftly applied the 3R Model as follows:[3]

Regret: Upfront, Deborah apologized sincerely and admitted her shortfalls. This showed empathy and created the safe space needed to build conversational trust.

Reason: She got to the core reasons (without excuses or blaming) why she and her team weren't delivering to plan. This showed positive vulnerability, and a willingness to engage.

Remedy: Deborah used powerful questions such as "What if ...?" which invited her client to explore and discover possible options together and co-create a solution.

From a neuroscience perspective, the 3Rs shifted the client's brain chemistry. Deborah's approach reduced the client's "fight response" by down-regulating his release of the stress hormone, cortisol, and increasing his release of the "bonding hormone," oxytocin.

Through this shift towards more "bonding," she successfully up-regulated trust levels with her client and got him operating from his Executive Brain (i.e., the prefrontal cortex) where trust levels are higher and more constructive conversations can take place.

By working together, she and her client co-created a solution: they both recognized the common interest of being committed to project delivery no matter what. With this, they combined their resources—the client's analytics team shared their expertise with Deborah's team and collaboratively they delivered the project.

For Deborah, there was no escaping late fee penalties, but this was made up more than tenfold in several future projects the same client commissioned with her team. From the brink of disaster, she successfully built a relationship based on trust, and the by-product was that her team became expert in digital profiling.

SECRET 7:

ASK POWERFUL QUESTIONS

The most successful people in life
are the ones who ask questions.

They're always learning.
They're always growing.

- Robert Kiyosaki

Questions can be powerful and can influence likability and relatedness. The more questions we ask about other people, the more people tend to like us.

But not all questions are created equally! Questions requiring a simple yes or no ("Did you get that project done?") are known as close-ended questions. Close-ended questions at best, don't inspire, and at worst can be toxic.

Instead, choose the more powerful open-ended question, ("Who?" "What?" "Where?" "Why?" "How?") which promotes growth and learning.

There is so much you want to ask team members. Yet, you know if you ask for an update or how their projects are going, they will say, "Fine," and you won't hear the whole story. Take a moment to formulate an open-ended question like, "What is working well?" or "How can the team's expertise help you further your group's goals (or solve a problem)?"

Successful people and leaders use powerful questions to elevate others (and themselves). Powerful questions enable them to clarify their thinking and therefore make better decisions—ones aligned with their goals and vision. Since successful people tend to have a propensity towards growth and often possess a growth mindset, they're likely to ask powerful questions from curiosity and an open mind. They're interested in discovering what they don't already know.

Successful leaders use powerful questions to:

- Challenge assumptions or potentially faulty thinking;

- Understand others better;

- Create solutions instead of roadblocks and problems;

- Explore new and innovative ideas, and;

- Identify gaps thinking and explore new possibilities.

A brief list of powerful questions successful leaders asks both themselves and others:

- What do I (you) really want?

- What assumptions am I (are you) making?

- How else can I (you) think about this?

- What truly matters here?

- What am I (are you) missing?

- What is possible here?

- What can I (we) learn from this?

- What is the other person thinking? (feeling? wanting? needing?)

- How can I (we) turn this into a win-win?

- How can I (we) help?

As Dale Carnegie advised in his 1936 classic, *How to Win Friends and Influence People*,

"Be a good listener. Ask questions the other person will enjoy answering." So, after you ask your open-ended question, make sure you listen to the answer. Successful leaders don't just ask powerful questions. They listen too!

CHAPTER TWO

The Language of Connection

You have applied and practiced the conversational secrets from the first chapter to strengthen trust. Still, you realize there is more to do. As a conscious leader, you recognize that when people miss deadlines, you will confront them, but you will do so while minding and nurturing your connections. You accomplish this by first listening with the intent to understand and by testing out assumptions. This is especially relevant during the pandemic when you worry about losing customers. But you remind yourself that people are being human, with all their vagaries and missteps (and you remember to include yourself in that conception of humanity). You don't avoid the difficult conversation (as you may have done in the past) about the impact and consequences of the missed deadline. In this conversation, you practice the conversational secrets below and regulate your own emotions so that you can work as a team.

It is particularly challenging now, but you stay conscious of the bigger and longer-term payoff: a healthy corporate culture. Attending to your connection with everyone increases motivation and prompts creativity, ultimately leading to a better overall outcome.

SECRET 8:

ADAPT LISTENING TO THE PURPOSE OF THE CONVERSATION

Most people do not listen with the intent to understand;

they listen with the intent to reply.

- Stephen Covey

Leaders often listen with the intent to reply rather than to understand the other's perspective, Covey says. The greatest speakers turn that tendency on its head. They listen to what the speaker is saying, thinking, and feeling with the intention to understand what is being communicated from the speaker's perspective.

Before Winston Churchill gave his famous address in Parliament that led Britain to join WWII, he deeply listened to the voice of the people. Churchill rode the London "Tube" and asked several people seated near him what they thought about whether Britain should enter the war. Their clear and heartfelt answers, that Britain must join in the effort, perhaps gave Churchill's speech to Parliament the passion and sense of conviction necessary to sway the nation.

Having engaged the public, he had the trust and will of the people standing alongside him that evening. When a leader listens deeply to people and they feel heard, the leader can experience the trust of the people which is the most precious asset people have to give a leader.

How can leaders level up their listening game?

There are three levels of listening a leader can use for effective conversations. (This concept is loosely adapted from the book, *Co-active Coaching*.)[4]

Level One:

The first level of listening is where many informational and transactional conversations occur. This is all about you as the listener. You listen to the information and how it impacts you internally. The rest of the time spent listening, you are thinking about what to say next and how you are going to say it. This is how many professional conversations take place, especially those that are primarily informational. Even during these types of conversations, it pays to listen more and speak less.

For example:

The CEO says, "We are implementing a new customer relationship management system, and I want everyone to start using it within a week."

As a senior leader listening to this, all you are thinking about is how you are going to tell your team that there is yet another new customer relationship management system for them to get used to. Everyone hated using the previous one. You don't think this will be different. You were just going to raise your hand and let the CEO know about the difficulty. You got distracted by a colleague for a moment and thankfully didn't say anything and continued to listen.

The CEO continues:

"I know you all must be groaning from the experience of the last CRM system. I am with you. These are some of the ways we are changing the implementation process, so we are successful this time. What additional ideas do you have?"

Level Two:

In the second level, you listen critically to discern whether you agree or disagree with what the speaker is saying. The goal is to understand well the other person's points so that you may sharpen your own counterpoints to influence the person to agree with you. The total focus is on understanding the other person. This can be useful in negotiations.

Example of Level Two listening:

You're having a conversation with an experienced CEO who is a supplier to your company and is trying to convince you, a millennial leader, to enter a strategic partnership that egregiously disadvantages your company. You think you understand his assumptions, so you boldly say,

"Look, from the offer you made, I realize, you must think either I have no experience, or that I am a pushover. I am the third generation in this business and have been learning from the ground up since I was 12 years old. Either we do this respectfully or I walk away."

As a millennial leader, you have deeply listened to this type of response from seasoned players and properly read the presumptions being made. They underestimate you and assume they can take advantage of you. You have learned to call out the assumptions and bend this toward your advantage in negotiations.

Level Three:

Level Three involves empathetic listening to the other person so that you may better understand the emotion and the feelings behind their spoken words. You tune in to their perspective, as you already understand your own perspective. This type of listening acknowledges that the other person is making perfect sense to himself and you want to understand how he's making sense from his point of view. The leadership secret to success here is to suspend one's judgement and/or agenda. Only then can the leader see someone else's point of view.

A broader perspective of Level Three listening acknowledges and considers the "field" and energy nonverbals (such as body language), and the emotion present in a communication. This is called "contextual" listening and is most effective in creating collaboration and innovation when both sides participate in active listening and focus on maximizing the outcome for both parties.

SECRET 9:

STOP AVOIDING

DIFFICULT CONVERSATIONS

Difficult conversations do not just involve feelings;

they are at their very core about feelings.

- Douglas Stone

Difficult conversations can feel toxic. It is common to avoid them. As a leader you can easily be tempted to do so, but it is rarely productive. Alternatively, you can become familiarized with the following effective ways to approach difficult conversations and gain confidence in handling them.

We want connection. We will need it to get to collaboration. But ignoring difficult issues will not make them go away and they will eventually impact negatively overall. At the very extreme, having that most difficult of conversations, the one which involves firing an employee, may be what's called for in order to allow for all the other vital connections to work, which is ultimately what makes a company thrive. Part of being in a leadership position involves the inevitability of having difficult conversations such as this, but for many, this can provoke dread. According to the research, firing an employee is one of the most difficult things a leader must do. It triggers anxiety and fear. As Douglas Stone points out in *Difficult Conversations,* one reason is that these conversations often contain strong emotions, and feelings can be messy and painful.[5] Have you ever had to fire a difficult employee—one who you know will yell and rant, or worse may break down and cry? Have you ever been in a heated team conversation that turned into a shouting match—one in which you wished you could be somewhere else?

Perhaps you even once imagined knocking people's heads together, or alternatively, as an introverted leader, running away. Both reactions involve a fight or flight response. This is what happens when our amygdala hijacks us. This part of the brain, in the limbic system, is much older than the more developed prefrontal cortex. The amygdala hijacks, or overwhelms, the executive function of the prefrontal cortex. The result of dreading and then circumventing difficult conversations is that the situation eventually builds to a breaking point. Avoiding a conversation that needs to be had often becomes an invitation for an angry outburst. An issue that was suppressed for too long, when it eventually emerges out in the open, can turn explosive. A Vital Smarts research study shows, that on average, delaying a difficult conversation at work will ultimately cost the company approximately $1,500 and eight hours of work time.[6]

Dr. Srini Pillay, neuroscientist, psychiatrist, and faculty at Harvard University executive education, suggests people can train their brain to overcome anxiety and fear. Telling your brain: "do not dread this difficult conversation," or "stop being afraid to confront your employee," is not effective when it comes to down-regulating strong emotions or feelings. According to Pillay, neuroscience suggests that when the brain is told no, or to stop, it is hardwired to not pay attention. This is a legacy gift of ancient hardwiring when humans needed to stay on high alert from predators.[7]

Pillay offers a combination that gives a person a fair chance at overcoming their fear and anxiety:

Having HOPE and BELIEF (that transcends fear) + ATTENDING (paying attention to the outcome you want) + COMMITMENT (holding yourself accountable for action), helps a person from getting unstuck from over-whelming emotion. Hope and belief win the fight with fear long enough for the executive function to have a shot at taking action. This translates to overcoming the tendency to avoid engaging in difficult conversations.

Stepping into Difficult Conversations:

What can you as a leader do to stop avoiding difficult conversations?

1. Stop shining the light on the dread or fear you have around the conversation.

2. Instead, focus on the outcome that you want the conversation to have.

3. Believe that you can do it.

4. The greater your commitment to the point at hand and the more actionable solutions you have, the easier it will become to enter difficult conversations.

Scenario Example:

You say to your direct report:

> "I know you gave Marie every opportunity to grow as a manager and everyone agrees she may be far more productive and happier as an individual contributor. I understand it is easier to avoid removing her from the management position, than to engage her in that difficult conversation. It can certainly be anxiety provoking as a first-time manager. Consider that Marie and her direct reports are suffering too. Let's meet and figure out together how you can stay calm and be true to yourself as a leader, while engaging Marie in a productive conversation that is both clear and caring."

SECRET 10:

SLOW DOWN, CHECK IN

Everything we hear is an opinion, not a fact.

Everything we see is a perspective, not the truth.

- Marcus Aurelius

Our brains have a vast capacity to store information and are constantly making new connections (new mental maps) while processing information. Most of the time, we update our mental maps subconsciously as this is energy efficient. Occasionally, we do so consciously, as in, when learning new skills, adopting new habits, and exploring unknown territory; but this takes a lot of (brain) energy.

Overall, we tend to behave on auto pilot—what Daniel Kahneman famously coined as *System 1 Thinking*: fast, unconscious, automatic, everyday decision, error prone.

We each experience life through a different lens and develop unique mental maps or views of the world. For example, two people watching the same movie can emerge from the theatre with very different reactions. One disliked the gratuitous violence (because they witnessed such violence in, say, a worn torn country), while the other was moved by the realism of the story (because it opened their eyes to something they'd never experienced).

Herein lies the challenge: Because our brains operate mostly on auto pilot (especially when under stress), when we are trying to help a colleague think through anything, we make the unconscious assumption that the other person's brain works the same as ours.[8] We explain connections or concepts that are obvious *to our mental map*, but don't exist to the same level or at all in the listener's mental map.

A study done at Stanford University found that 90% [!] of conversations miss their mark; a "lost in translation" experience between two mental maps. Fundamentally, no two people have the same mental maps by which they navigate life.

Against this backdrop, in today's fast paced 24/7 connected world, leaders are under a tremendous amount of stress to deliver fast. They easily fall into System 1 Thinking (the energy efficient and less conscious way). On top of that, being in a position of power, they often get stuck in "being addicted to being right"; they enquire and then advocate the way (their way) forward, occasionally offering some compromise.[9] This might be efficient in the moment, but it is hugely error prone—sometimes with devastating consequences.

Great leaders recognize the power of the expression "seek to understand to be understood" and know when to practice the art of slowing down and checking in (which involves switching off their autopilot).

Slowing down as an effective mode may sound counter-intuitive, but it allows for strategic and emotional alignment upfront and saves tremendous time later. If there are alignment issues, they're likely to catch up with you eventually and you will find yourself having to back up and correct mistakes in a way that will probably be even more time consuming.

What does 'slow down, check in' look like in practice?

Leaders who master this art deliberately slow their pace. They notice their breathing in order to get centered. They become present to the moment by tuning out distractions and focus on what is important now. Only then do they engage in conversations where they:

- Suspend their agenda and listen to connect without judging or rejecting ideas.

- Probe the meaning of words used and ideas being presented to develop a shared mental map or understanding.

- Test their assumptions without holding attachments to anything.

- Paraphrase: "What I'm hearing you say is ..." to close gaps in understanding.

- Stay curious and courageously ask questions for which they do not have the answer.

- Seek alignment in meetings by asking upfront, "What would a successful meeting look like today?"

Ultimately, by consciously slowing down and checking in, great leaders support others in thinking for themselves so that they take ownership to drive plans forward.

SECRET 11:

BEWARE—MOVIES OF THE MIND

What you think you become.
What you feel you attract.
What you imagine you create.

- Natalie Ledwell

What are Movies of the Mind? It is worth a leader's while to meditate on this because changing one's mind movies exponentially transforms conversations. Visualize an old film reel that runs on tape. The tape unwinds and the movie plays on the big screen. Consider, as a leader, how easy it is to become immersed in the movie's reality even though it is not real. That is what happens in the brain. The tape gets played repeatedly, creating grooves in the same neural pathways. It is much like a needle stuck in a groove on a vinyl album that spins around an old RCA turntable.

The movies in the mind stay stuck at the time the neural pathways were first created. What these pathways all have in common is that they set limiting beliefs in our mind on what we can and can't do or what we can achieve or be. These pathways are usually set way below our actual potential. Every five seconds our brain is asking, "Is this friend or foe; are we safe or not?" Out of the tens of thousands of thoughts a day, the majority are negative thoughts. This negativity bias comes with hardwiring inherited from our ancestors whose minds imprinted this mode which saved them from predators. What is so dangerous about being stuck in the "groove" of the negative mind movies is that they're unconscious. They're part of you, like the air you breathe—but not nearly as helpful!

As a leader, how can changing your mind movies change your conversations?

Scenario Example:

Finding your voice in conversations with the CEO, despite being a top performer and an emerging leader, doesn't come easily.

Daphne was called in by the CEO for a meeting about the status of a high-profile project. The CEO's brusque approach unconsciously triggered memories of Daphne being on the receiving end of constant criticism. She felt suddenly sapped of her creativity and confidence. Her report ended up sounding far less promising than what she originally concluded about the figures that she walked in with.

What was meant to spur performance, instead, triggered feelings of never being good enough. You think that your good work speaks for itself and demur from opportunities of moving up in the company. "If I deserved the promotion, wouldn't I have gotten it already?" you tell yourself. Anxiety, fear, and the neurochemical, cortisol, that these reactions release, shut down the Executive Brain (i.e., the prefrontal cortex), leaving you in a full "amygdala hijack," where your unregulated emotions are in control.

In the above scenario, the CEO translated Daphne's overly deferential and timid interaction as a lack of confidence and became ambivalent about promoting her upwards. This anxiety and the fear, and the limiting belief of not being good enough that it subconsciously generates, is keeping this talented woman tongue-tied and is impacting her ability to get promoted.

How can you utilize the awareness of this dynamic to self-coach towards strength as an emerging leader?

1. Awareness:

Understand that there are subconscious movies of the mind being played that hold people back from achieving their goals. These movies with their internalized chatter represent "your thinking about your thinking." They're narratives constructed by you and the good news is, they can be *reconstructed* by you. Use the power of reflection to step back and ask yourself by what you are being triggered when it comes to speaking with the CEO.

Perhaps the CEO triggers you whenever he goes into his brusque "business mode." Once you reflect on and identify your triggers, the awareness alone of why you freeze or refrain from asking for a promotion, is half the battle. Knowing takes away the intensity—the pressure cooker experience of having no clue as to why your brain is hijacking your normally rational self. Awareness alone, however necessary, isn't sufficient.

2. Choice:

You have a choice, and you can exercise it fully or not. Even in not choosing (doing nothing) you are making a choice. You can equally make the choice that these limiting beliefs do not remain in the driver's seat—you are. Once aware of the trigger, you have the choice, for example, to do deep breathing to calm your body before going into the CEO's office. You can choose a reminder affirmation, for example, that you are an adult, and any criticism is a learning experience. There is nothing to fear, just a learning opportunity taking place. You are now aware and have made a choice. The next step is to harness your intention.

3. Intention:

Telling your brain to stop thinking about negative thoughts doesn't work. The brain is hardwired to disregard such instructions. Your brain, however, is more likely to comply when asked to replace the negative behavior with something positive.

In this example of preparing to go in to see the CEO, instead of self-coaching by saying, "stop being so anxious," a leader can say, "I am a top performer. I am doing fine. I can even ask for the promotion." Having awareness, making a choice, and setting one's intention on a good track, bring a person only halfway. *Acting* on the awareness, choice, and intention is what exponentially changes negative mind movies into positive ones that can work on your behalf.

4. Act:

When you act by finding your voice and learn to ask for what you want, oxytocin, the "feel good bonding hormone," is released (instead of the stress hormone, cortisol). Oxytocin reinforces the learning loop. Going in to speak to the CEO with the positive mindset the first time may be difficult. However, with the learning loop in effect, the conversation gets easier over time. You may be surprised to find that you speak up more easily in team meetings, that people notice your good ideas, and that your competence and confidence have "suddenly" grown.

Six months later, the above-mentioned leader got her promotion. Intention and choice are necessary, and it is taking action by replacing the old mind movies with positive mind movies that propels change forward toward desired results.

SECRET 12:

MANAGE FEAR CENTRAL—
WHICH BRAIN IS IN CHARGE?

Bad news sells because the amygdala
is always looking for something to fear.

- Peter Diamandis

The amygdala is housed in the limbic brain, the seat of emotions. Dubbed, "Fear Central" by the neuroscientist, Joseph LeDoux, the amygdala is thought of as the seat of the "fight or flight" response. It is the early warning system, hardwired in the brain to protect humans from physical threats. The amygdala, always on the lookout for something to fear, often wins out over the prefrontal cortex, the thinking, mature, or Executive Brain that helps navigate decisions. The brain, however, can't distinguish between physical and social threats, and real or imagined threats.

To this end, Daniel Kahneman found that that the brain hates losing, twice as much as it likes winning. In other words, we're twice as likely to lean towards the closed-mindedness of "Fear Central" than towards the open-mindedness of our Executive Brain, or the prefrontal cortex.

When a leader provides critical feedback to an employee in front of colleagues—regardless of the intention—they should realize the following: that employee will experience the social threat of being shamed in front of other colleagues as being more painful than a physical threat. When one receives critical feedback, no matter how benignly it is presented, the brain experiences it as an attack, perceives it as negative, and shuts down. To maintain (and even nurture) the connections that are the fabric of your organization, you, as the leader, will need to attend to this fact. Neuroscience has proven that the adage of "sticks and stones can break my bones, but words can never harm me" is false.

When the amygdala perceives social threat, the neurochemical cortisol is released, and people experience stress. Humans can manage rising cortisol levels on an occasional basis as it is designed for coping with intermittent danger. When cortisol levels remain constantly high, it leads to a state of anxiety and is even physically detrimental. Let's face it: most of the work today gets done through conversations. When leaders create an environment, through their conversations in which employees constantly experience stress, and where fear is generated, the resulting stress and anxiety negatively impacts people emotionally and physically.

What can a leader do?

A leader can, firstly, have the meeting behind closed doors (which relieves the person from fear of being shamed in front of colleagues) and secondly, open the discussion using Marshall Goldsmith's "feedforward" approach.[10] The leader can say: "Rather than looking backwards and giving feedback, how about we talk about what would be useful going forward?" Right away, the brain moves from fear about being criticized (limbic system) to wrapping the mind around something it can do (prefrontal cortex). The result is that the employee relaxes and becomes more open to learning.

Metacognition, or the ability to think about thinking, sets humans apart. Thoughts have the capacity to manage emotions which can come in handy for a leader during difficult conversations. Yet, it can be very tough as a leader or manager to zip-it and stay grounded when someone provokes you in a conversation. With provocation, commonly, a person takes the bait, despite knowing it is not a wise move.

As a leader, learn what flips your switch and replace it with something that allows the prefrontal cortex the chance to engage its smarts.

1. Become aware of your emotional triggers. What are your hot buttons?

2. Once aware of the actions, words, and triggers that set you off, take five deep breaths, count sheep, flick a rubber band on your wrist, or anything that takes 7-10 seconds. This will give time for the prefrontal cortex to kick in. Think of this activity as breaking the circuit that defuses the situation.

Scenario Example:

Several leadership team members decide to stonewall the CEO's transformation initiative. They think the change applies to the rest of the company, just not their divisions. Katy, the CEO, gets word that some team members think this is just "another flavor of the month." They have been quietly sabotaging efforts by doing nothing to move the effort forward. Furious, Katy has the urge to take off her pump and pound the table with it like Premier Khrushchev did with his shoe during the Cold War. Katy thinks to herself, "Let them know who the boss is once and for all." Then she smiled to herself. "That would be funny since none of the millennials on the team probably have a clue who Khrushchev was."

Neuroscience research provides evidence that there is on only .07 of a second between the trigger event, and when the amygdala kicks in and sounds the alarm for an amygdala hijack to occur. Leaders must be self-aware of their triggers and regulate their emotions to keep the amygdala from hijacking their normally rational brain.

The amygdala is millions of years old in comparison to the infant prefrontal cortex. When the amygdala and basal ganglia (the brain of the autonomic nervous system or the reptilian brain which is even more ancient) get together they have the power to shut down the younger thinking brain. This explains how when intense emotions are involved—whether in love, or anger, or feeling betrayed—rational decision making often takes a backseat. Katy self-coached herself, knowing this was a hot button issue as it could be experienced as a threat and a test of her leadership as a woman. Ahead of time, she practiced being mindful, took a few breaths to calm down her anxiety, and allowed her thinking brain to be in the driver seat. She decided not to avoid the difficult conversation and rather, focused on the outcome of unifying the team and having them hold each other accountable.

Katy called out the issue at the next team meeting:

> "I hear that several of you think the transformation initiative will blow over, so, you haven't yet begun to move it forward. Today we have an opportunity to bring any issues forward that may have delayed progress. Let us know what help or resources you need from me and your colleagues around the table to succeed. We are all in this together. A hole in one part of our boat sinks all of us. And, as a reminder, the good news is, your leadership during this transformation process will inform your future and compensation in the company. Now let us get down to work."

Katy looked around at the faces on the team. "Okay," she thought to herself, "they got the message." Having first composed herself, she was able to convey the message effectively—and in her own style. This not being her first rodeo, Katy knew that for change to be successful, she needed to provide the right administrative and infrastructural climate for people to take the transformation seriously.

SECRET 13:

EXPRESS YOUR THOUGHTS POSITIVELY

Handle them carefully,
for words have more power than atom bombs.

- Pearl Strachan Hurd

There are two boys climbing a tree when suddenly there's a huge gust of wind. One of the mothers watching yells out to her son, "Hang on tight!" while the other mother yells, "Don't fall!" Because our minds are programmed to subconsciously follow the direction of our words, the word, "fall" stood out when his mother cautioned, "Don't fall" and he fell from the tree. It was the focus of the action, rather than the modifiers around the word that made the strongest impression—and the imagery of falling, in this case, made the strongest impression.

Words change worlds. From a leadership perspective, and in everyday life for that matter, leaders who project themselves using positive words, matching tone, and body language, gain more influence and persuasive power. They come across with more confidence, have better connections with others, and perhaps not surprisingly, more opportunities open for them. Studies show that positive statements are estimated to be understood 30–40% times faster than negative ones. So, in addition to facilitating team comprehension, there is the bonus that the leader's words are well received!

We can learn from Shakespeare when Hamlet said, "There is nothing either good or bad, but thinking it makes it so." When we choose to express ourselves positively (to ourselves and to others), over time, our quality of life improves, and we nurture a happier mindset. Leaders with such mindsets are likely to create a more positive climate in which teams can consistently perform successfully and recover more quickly from failure. This provides a significant competitive advantage.

Martin Luther King famously said, "I have a dream!" Imagine if he had spoken like a typical business leader and said, "I have a plan!" No one would have been inspired to listen further.

Overall, there's a magical feeling we experience when in the company of positive leaders. They somehow make us feel better about ourselves, they nurture a happy mindset, and they help us see new possibilities in business and in life.

The power of positive framing bias was famously demonstrated in an experiment designed by the cognitive and mathematical psychologist Amos Tversky and 2002 Nobel Memorial Prize winner in Economic Sciences, Daniel Kahneman.[11]

Eerily, given the Covid-19 situation afflicting the world today, participants were asked to choose between two treatments for 600 people affected by a deadly disease. Both treatments were framed either in a positive frame or a negative frame. Treatment A provided a certain outcome of saving 200 lives and 400 will die. Treatment B provided probability outcomes, of a 33% chance that all 600 would live and a 66% chance that all 600 would die.

Framing	Treatment A	Treatment B
Positive	Saves 200 lives	A 33% chance of saving all 600 people, 66% possibility of saving no one
Negative	400 people will die	A 33% chance that no people will die, 66% probability that all 600 will die

Tversky and Kahneman's experiment showed that the certain gain in Treatment A was chosen by 72% of participants when it was presented with positive framing ("Saves 200 lives"). Conversely, when Treatment A was presented with negative framing ("400 people will die"), it was chosen by only 22% of participants, who preferred their probabilistic chances ("66% probability that all 600 will die").

Framing your ideas and vision in a positive frame inspires and engages others into action and decision, and to follow your lead.

SECRET 14:

LEAN INTO CONVERSATIONAL AND EMOTIONAL AGILITY

---

*Our key to transforming anything
lies in our ability to reframe it.*

- Marianne Williamson

Successful leaders are agile conversationalists, often mediating and navigating a conversation to a new ending. They know when and how to shape the conversation in a more productive, positive, or profitable direction.

They don't merely respond or react emotionally to what others are saying or doing. Rather, they use their skills and energy to lead emotions and the conversation in a new direction. Successful people help others move from being stuck in resistance to being open and engaging more meaningfully.

For example, one of our clients turned around a tense and high-value negotiation when she acknowledged the pressure both parties were feeling on pricing due to the economic downturn. She refocused both her team and the other side on the long-term outcome benefits to ensuring that both sides emerge financially strong and able to continue doing business together.

There are three Rs that constitute the primary skills to transform a conversation, shift its direction, and lead to a better outcome.

Reframe: This means to place something in a new frame of reference, to assign a new meaning or context, to see the situation from a different perspective.[12]

> Reframing can open the other person's view from being closed, negative, or judgmental and help shift it towards a positive, more open frame that feels safer to new opinions.

> A simple example: Reframe "This is a problem" by asking, "What are several ways we might achieve our goal here?" This question helps to redirect focus away from the problem and towards a solution.

Refocus: This involves shifting the focus of attention onto something different, i.e., from narrow conclusions or assumptions to seeing new connections and possibilities.

> Part of the brain is designed for focusing which is helpful when we are seeking something or working to get something done. Focusing intently on something can become *unhelpful* when we miss seeing the bigger picture, context, or consequences.

> Leaders can guide others to refocus their intention onto what is important and towards that which matters most for achieving a desired outcome.

> A simple example: Refocus "That'll never work!" to "Let's look at what has worked well already."

Redirect: To guide others to a different thinking path, i.e., from an emotionally stuck position to seeing new possibilities and opportunities.

A simple example: Redirect "I'm just not good at this" to "You are good at lots of other things. How did you get good at those things?" Such a question can help a person shift from the unproductive and uncreative state of feeling incompetent to a path of ongoing learning or development and the possibility of seeking outside help.

CHAPTER THREE

The Language of Collaboration

You are beginning to see how developing trust and connection is having an impact on people. People seem more at ease knowing where you stand and where the company is going, especially regarding what directly impacts them.

The Pandemic continues, and as a leader you want to assert your authority as everyone is working remotely. You are about to talk to your thousands of employees. You clear your throat to muster an authoritative presence. All this trust and connection you worked hard to create is good, and more is needed; your team needs you to show up as a leader—of the people and for the people.

You stop for a moment to take a deep breath and remind yourself how powerful the words of a leader are, and how toxic conversations can be that personify power over people. When you engender trust and connection you are powerful—but it needs to be with people rather than over people. So, you switch your tone and language to the authentic and heartfelt you.

Your words resonate and people are moved by your candor. You smile to yourself and set a calendar reminder to review the other conversational secrets in this chapter so you can start practicing them more regularly for even greater leadership impact.

SECRET 15:

LEVERAGE MODERN POWER

What counts is the way power is used—
whether with swagger and contempt
or with prudence, discipline, and magnanimity.
What counts is the purpose for which power is used—
whether for aggrandizement or for liberation.

- John F. Kennedy

Modern, successful leaders understand that power is dynamic. Fluid. Both given and earned. Multi-dimensional.

Traditional views of power are based in sources of authority, position, wealth, and ownership—the power and rights of kings, queens, and the landed gentry. Such notions of "Power Over" are rooted in scarcity: you have it, or they have it. Today's leadership is not a zero-sum game.

Power Over. Post Industrial Revolution notions of power retained the power of leading from authority and position; as employees gained collective power through unionization and democratic voting practices, power continued to be exercised in organizations and governments as Power-Over through position and authority.

In the Information and Technology Age, authority from position and title has proven no longer sufficient to lead teams and organizations effectively.

Modern leaders stumble and fail when they lead from an I-Centric place and view sharing power as a sign of weakness.

Like Jae. When Jae presents at the leadership summit, he constantly mentions his own accomplishments without highlighting those of his staff sitting in the audience who were the ones who really did the work. He doesn't notice (or perhaps care) that his team members are inattentive, looking at email on their phones or checking the time.

Today, successful, and effective companies are transitioning to ...

Power With. Modern successful leaders are 'We-Centric' and invite others to take the lead, sharing power through encouraging and supporting others to build their leadership. As a We-Centric leader, invite team members to take ownership on a project, to lead a segment of your team meetings.

Power To. Successful people have exercised their power to choose and to act in a consistent and regular manner. And successful leaders ensure that there is an atmosphere that encourages the Power To, which is rooted in action and based in choice. Power To is expansive and available to everyone, regardless of formal authority, or power derived from position.[13]

The #MeToo movement is a clear, modern example of both Power To combined with Power With, persuading an entire generation towards action and choice. Many traditional leaders who wielded Power Over to achieve their success have now lost their positions of power and authority, and in some cases, even their liberty.

SECRET 16:

PRACTICE "YES, AND ..."

In the long history of humankind (and animal kind too)
those who learned to collaborate
and improvise most effectively have prevailed.

- Charles Darwin

If Bill Gates had listened to the naysayers expressing things like, "That'll never happen," we wouldn't have personal computers or even our smartphones.

Our reptile brains LOVE certainty. Status quo. Safety. Yet in our VUCA 21st Century world, Uncertainty is more the rule of the day. Leading from Authority, or the "command and control" approach, is no longer enough to get people to new actions, behavior, or results.

Rather, the increasing imperative in business to compete in the marketplace is to innovate and collaborate.

We can take a cue from a fundamental practice in improvisational theatre, where "Yes, and ..." means accepting every single offer and building on it. In improvisational theatre, a scene is created when actors accept what the other has said or done ("yes") and add their own words and actions ("and"). In that manner, "yes and ..." becomes the prompt which moves the scene forward. The scene doesn't move forward if the idea is suppressed or rejected.

Sound familiar? "That'll never happen" is a rejection of an idea. Like hearing "Yes BUT ..." the great conversation eraser. We might thank Bill Gates that he listened to another cast of characters instead.

When you employ "Yes, and ..." the other person feels heard. They hear their idea accepted. Acceptance doesn't mean you agree to run the whole way with it. Your turn is next! Add your thought or idea—and something new is created. Notice in your conversations how this small addition may reap great dividends.

And beware: Going for the "and" requires an open mind, and the willingness to seek ways to build on what is presented.

Secrets to help you collaborate and improvise by trading "Yes, but ..." with "Yes, and ...":

1. "But" out. When you catch your thoughts or your mouth saying, "Yes, **but**" practice catching yourself, and switching gears to saying (and thinking), "Yes, **and**" and see what comes next.

2. Brainstorm with only one rule: you can only add a new idea, not reject an idea. Notice what comes up. Usually, it's the weird and wonderful juxtaposed with the ordinary that provides the humor in Improv, and the exceptional innovative idea when brainstorming.

SECRET 17:

LET GO OF ADDICTED TO BEING RIGHT

Out beyond the ideas of wrongdoing and right-doing
there is a field.
I'll meet you there.

- Rumi

There were no weapons of mass destruction.[14] And yet, the unwavering commitment to the original statement that there were WMDs had the very high cost of trillions of dollars and thousands of lives lost.

While starting a war may be on the extreme end of the high cost of the addiction to being right, the everyday costs are breakdowns in conversations, relationships, and organizations. Addiction to being right typically leads to a telling or yelling style, a positional stance, or, in certain environments, high authoritarian (bordering on dictatorial) leadership.

Being addicted to being right makes other people wrong. When one is easily offended, it can be an indication of being addicted to being right. Being right with absolute certainty keeps the focus on the "I" leader (even when it is exercised under the guise of "helping the team succeed"). It is the "I" who is right, not the "We" in the team.

Being positional is different from taking a stand. Positional precludes other possibilities from also being true. It is an almost obsessive attachment to position over interests.

When you fight for your way (the "right" way) you may feel the rush of adrenaline and endorphins and get a sense of achievement, even triumph. At the same time, the other person is likely to feel the very opposite brain chemicals of fear and distrust which will stir up defensiveness. While you get high off your dominance, they can feel diminished, demeaned, and devalued as the distrust and fear centers of their brain get activated.

The invisible costs of being right are disengagement and the resulting diminishment of collaboration and innovation.

As Simon Sinek outlined in The Infinite Game, the costs can be pervasive and at the highest levels:

> "There was good reason for the silence. The executives were scared. Prior to [new Ford Motor Company CEO] Mullaly, the former CEO would regularly berate, humiliate or fire people who told him things he didn't want to hear...executives were now conditioned to hide problem areas or missed financial targets to protect themselves from the CEO."[15]

Successful leaders understand they don't have all the answers all the time and they listen to others' viewpoints; they course correct as new information is considered. With the broadened understanding these leaders get from listening to others, they can create a vision of shared success and communicating with clarity and transparency.

SECRET 18:

TEST YOUR ASSUMPTIONS TO RESOLVE CONFLICTS

If we all worked on the assumption
that what is accepted as true
is really true, there would be little hope of advance.

- Orville Wright

It is logical for leaders to use rational arguments to persuade others to their point of view in a conflict. Yet as Jonathan Swift noted, you can never reason anyone into something unless they already believed in that rational argument. Rational arguments don't always work, in part because we don't deal with the underlying emotions nor do we test the assumptions on which they're based. The following frustrating scenario gets played out daily in leadership teams around the world.

Scenario Example:

Participants on a leadership team find themselves in a heated argument over which strategy to pursue for the following year. Marketing and manufacturing have each pitched their rational arguments back and forth as in a ping pong match, frustrating everyone on the team. It is as if they're not listening to one another and are only interested in their own points of view. Sarah, the leader, becomes a referee, and everyone turns to her for a decision. She's unsure of what to do to guide the meeting productively.

What can leaders of these teams do?

The wise leader recognizes that in many conversations, the root of the conflict lies in *differences about assumptions*—what they mean, and what to do about them. "Testing your assumptions" is a conversational power tool. It is designed to remove obstacles and move conversations forward. Both of the following steps are equally important:

The first step is to prime the team by creating the environment in which the team can thrive. Sarah primed the team with "Guidelines for Engagement," or ways in which the team agree to treat each other so they can do their best work. Integrity, transparency, all voices respected and heard, civility, and no raised voices were all part of their operating principles.

Sarah suggested the team add "Test your assumptions" to the list. She explained: "I think all members of the team are in 'violent agreement' throughout all the chaos of the back-and-forth arguments. We can go back to the beginning and create scaffolding from where John made the proposal. From there, we can implement the tool of testing the assumptions of the proposal to cut through the noise and chaos and get to the crux of the issue."

The team, while remaining somewhat doubtful, was glad to get a break from the bickering and agreed.

Could a simple practice such as this make a difference?

Sarah asked John to lay out the assumptions underlying his proposal. The team had gone down this path before. What was different this time, however, was that they all got to voice how they had heard the proposal. In doing so, they realized that this was the point at which the disagreement for all the team members had occurred, and now they got clarity. The fundamental differences that now surfaced had their source with how they interpreted the assumptions.

John shook his head in disbelief. There was agreement on just about everything, but no wonder his colleagues were so adamantly opposed. John would be too, given their interpretation of just one assumption that hadn't been clarified. John had assumed that everyone heard his explanation of the 25% reduction in resources that he had up on the slides. He was sure he had explained it as reducing marketing expenses, but he hadn't intended that people would assume he really meant headcount.

Once the group aligned around both the marketing and manufacturing **assumptions and their meanings,** they were able to work things through. From then on, the team learned to test assumptions in a collaborative way, early in a proposal process. Now that they got the hang of testing the assumptions in an open-minded, non-judgmental way, the team had a good-natured laugh together. They agreed with Sarah that John and the team had been in "violent agreement" all along; they just didn't know it at the time.

In this example we can see how as a leader you can move from a telling, or dictating, to a "share and discovery" approach of each other's assumptions. It might look something like this:

> "In our conversation today, I won't tell you what we should do. We will approach this conversation with a growth mindset, expanding how we think and by staying open and ready to learn new ideas from each other's perspectives. Maybe we missed something. We can look beyond the one or two options on the table. Let's test our assumptions together and make sure we come to the best possible decision."

SECRET 19:

EXPLORE "WHAT IF ...?" QUESTIONS

The two least developed skills in the workplace:
the ability to have uncomfortable conversations
and ask, 'what if' questions.

- Judith E. Glaser

Like an ostrich with its head in the sand, trying to innovate with old solutions often results in more of the same—or mud in your eye. Neuroscience helps explain why. Our brains are inherently lazy. There is only so much information the brain can handle, so, "objective" heuristics are often used in the decision-making process. Neural pathways get created and the brain gets very comfortable accepting those decisions as the right ones. What happens, however, when there are problems for which there are no answers?

As a leader, how can the powerful "What if" question create conversations that exponentially accelerate change?

Scenario Example:

As the CEO, you are painfully aware that the company must pivot from its current identity as a "grow" organization of marijuana. The margins aren't sustainable for the long term. The marketplace is young and dynamic, moving rapidly, and money is burning too quickly.

You bring your team together for a conversation:

"We know where the marketplace is trending and where it is heading in two years. We know our competitors and gaps in the marketplace. We know our strengths and weaknesses. We know our financials and we all agree we must pivot; it's now or never. We have questions, that have no answers. What do we pivot to? How do we do it? We are pioneers in the field, paving the path for others. Forget the expensive consultants. The best minds in the business are sitting here. Today we are going to use a compact 'power tool' (a whirring sound is made for effect) to figure out how to pivot our company. It requires that we suspend all judgment. It requires that we open our minds to new possibilities we never would have considered before. The power tool is two words: 'WHAT IF.'

The team members chuckle quietly under their breath. They love how the CEO always pulls a rabbit out of a hat at just the right time. The CEO divides the team into three small groups, standing around a flipchart and hands them large 4x6 sticky notes to start working on how to pivot the company.

"What if" presents leaders with a powerful means to move conversations and innovation forward. Why is that? It is because these two words, "What if":

- Awaken the brain to new ways of thinking.

- Help the brain suspend judgment.

- Help people think about their thinking instead of automatically responding.

- Encourage us to consider different possibilities.

- Develop new neural pathways—grooves that can accommodate new decisions (which then become embedded into memory).

Let's continue with our CEO

The CEO asked the groups standing around the flip charts with sticky notes to consider:

- "What if we pivoted to becoming a Cannabis extraction instead of a grow company?"

- "What if we created an educational programming platform to supplement growth?"

- 'What if we took our grow knowledge, and as a team, hired ourselves out to one of the big operations?"

- "What if we became consultants to other start-ups?"

- "Go wild with your own other 'What ifs'."

And so, the day workshop ended on a high note of possibility. The next day of the pivoting workshop, the energy in the room was palpable. Each idea had its own airing with the team.

- What if your assumptions about the market, money, competition are right?

- What if some of the assumptions regarding the financials, customer base etc. aren't accurate? How does that change the forecast?

The CEO had set the stage with a small power tool that allowed for assumptions to be tested, all ideas to be heard without judgment, and for a deep bond of trust to forge among the members. At the end of the third day, the team emerged bleary eyed—but they had a plan. It was none of the original ideas. The winning strategy emerged out of the deep informal dialogue on the second evening when they were eating dinner together.

What do you think they decided to do?

Jason swallowed hard. He got up and pushed his chair back from the table.

"Now we sell weed. By 2022 we will have three income streams. First, we will research and overhaul our current product by planting, harvesting, and branding ourselves as growing the best organic weed in the country. Second, rather than spend money on acquiring more land to grow product, we will raise venture capital to buy land all over the country which we will rent to growers like ourselves. In this way, we will be in the real estate business making residual money that doesn't depend on our crop. The third change that emerged is that, for the first time, we will have to brand our weed, so we can sell by quality rather than quantity and that will take us back to the R&D lab to differentiate ourselves."

A hush fell over the room. The CEO thought for a minute. He was so proud of his team. Even if they didn't implement all three, these were all great ideas, and he knew they had potentially struck gold.

SECRET 20:

BE STRONGER THAN YOUR EXCUSES

Accountability is the glue that bonds commitment to results.

- Will Craig

What is it about the word "accountability" that makes it intimidating? Likely, it's about the vulnerability of being seen, judged, or found deficient in some area. Perhaps there was a deadline passed, an agreement neglected, or some blunder made that is difficult to face.

Lack of accountability has been found to be a key factor—and perhaps *the* factor—in failed leadership attempts to navigate fluid political-socio-economic business environments.

There is no escaping it then! To be successful as a leader—and we're all leaders—keeping yourself and others accountable is critical. Accountability **is** what allows a great vision to be realized. While we may need to stretch ourselves in this area, consistent accountability brings our team and even our society into a new world of possibilities. Over time, it also builds that magic ingredient of **trust** in leaders and organizations as they model reliability. This, in turn, nurtures the organization's reputation.

Leaders can take on an "adaptive coaching leadership" style by leaning into the emotional intelligence competencies. This is what's called Leader as Coach.[16] They encourage the development of empathy and self-awareness and bring accountability to the surface with team members. This is how to create high performing future-fit leaders who then go on to influence high performance teams, who then influence high performance organisations.

A Leader as Coach also knows how to suspend their own agenda(s) and get furiously curious. Curiosity opens the door to the collaborative process for their team members in developing and co-creating accountability. Now, with the team an integrative part of the process towards the goal, the Leader as Coach can follow-up within the spirit of accountability as a tool for action and learning and not for passing judgment. Then they can all get down to business with a collaborative mindset:

- What do the results look like?

- What worked well and what didn't?

- What's the learning for next time?

- What is the best way to move forward?

Scenario Example:

Ted was recently promoted to Retail Practice Head in a large global consulting firm. For the first time in his career, he wasn't only asked to be "responsible for," but to become "accountable for" securing new client accounts—and this in a turbulent Covid-19 driven retail environment.

Ted felt an immense sense of pressure to deliver, and his limbic brain took over. He went into protect mode (fight, flight, freeze, or appease) and started to recklessly chase every single lead. After a few months of failing to deliver, the stress on him and the team was becoming evident. Something needed to change.

Ted met with his line manager Christy. She first created a safe environment for them to both explore, discover, and share without judgment. Christy asked Ted powerful questions to which she didn't have the answers. Christy explored areas in Ted's life where he felt competent and successful. Ted was an avid surfer and what emerged was a surfing metaphor to guide Ted (and his team) forward.

With Christy's support, he moved into a more confident state (which calmed his limbic brain) by borrowing a "surfing" perspective from which to find his solution for driving sales. He recognized that he was surfing an ocean of opportunity and he needed to assess each wave with a studied approach and only surf those that would deliver higher chances of a great ride.

He took the surfing analogy further: At the end of the day, he just needed to sit on the beach with his surfboard planted in the sand, and reflect: "What worked for me/us today? What did I/we do that got in my/our way? What do I/we need to change for tomorrow?"

To bring the accountability piece alive, Ted brought his surfboard to the office (it became a permanent fixture), shared the story, and allowed his team to co-create a new sales strategy. Within six months, Ted and his team were on track to being counted among the "Top 3" best performing sales teams in the business globally—a "surfing goal" they had set for themselves and announced publicly.

In adopting this process, Ted was making himself *stronger than his excuses.*

While he took away many lessons from this experience, his most important lesson learned about accountability and driving results was this:

Your 'surfing' will improve 50% when you publicly announce your goals.

SECRET 21:

CREATE THE CLIMATE FOR COLLABORATION

Never doubt that a small group of thoughtful,
committed people can change the world.
Indeed. It is the only thing that ever has.

- Margaret Mead

In our introduction, we referred to the converging of the economic, biological (pandemic), and social crisis. Redesigning conversations is a tool that effective leaders can embed in their organizational cultures. Regenerative conversations can prepare teams to transform organizations. They can help organizations move from a primarily shareholder-centric perspective to a more human-centered one, where all stakeholders benefit.

Conversations during the pandemic have helped organizations reach their tipping point to topple the hegemony of the biological and economic model of survival of the fittest. Andreas Weber suggests that the influential dual bio-economic model has been the primary value driver in the modern industrial era.

The biological part of bio-economics refers to Darwin's biological theory of "survival of the fittest" as a species. The economic part of bio-economics Weber refers to, is how capitalism's primary perspective is that those who take the risks by putting their money into companies, i.e., shareholders, should benefit the most. And the number one job of companies is to compete in the marketplace and make money for shareholders. There is always a clear winner and loser in a fixed pie. We see the extreme version of this today where the gap between those who have and those who do not is greater than at any time in history.

The pandemic, at this juncture of history has unexpectedly provided an incredible opportunity, if we take it, to close the inequality gap. Many corporations and individuals have begun to identify with what Virginia Burden has said, "Cooperation is an intelligent functioning of the concept of laissez faire—a thorough conviction that nobody can get there unless everybody gets there."[17] These are the types of conversations we want to prepare our leaders to have.

The research of economists, biologists, climatologists, and other scientists have recognized and extrapolated that the human species has evolved from diversification through competitiveness, to integration through collaboration to optimize the whole system. New biological research is showing a more fundamentally complex and interdependent model at the cellular level rather than survival of the fittest. Weber suggests that rather than competing for resources, nature's economic paradigm has also been to share the abundance that exists in the system.[18]

What works for evolution can work for the economy and social change. The economy too, according to Daniel Wahl,[19] can be redesigned so that competition and collaboration aren't mutually exclusive, but rather can be used at the right time, in the right way, to create abundance for all of society, not just the privileged few.

How can we prepare teams to have regenerative types of conversations to build high performance teams and organizations that support evolved organizational systems that flourish through trust, connection and collaboration across all stakeholders? Follow the obvious secrets below that leaders don't use often enough in conversations with their teams, and you will get there.

1. Create an environment of psychological safety and trust within the team.

    a. This creates the capacity for people to share openly, stop hoarding information, start asking for help, and admit mistakes. In Google's Project Aristotle study on what makes for effective teams, the researchers found that psychological safety was the leading indicator (rather than technical abilities). When you have psychological safety, then trust and connection develop more easily.

2. Develop a Compelling Purpose

    a. As a leader, create a draft of what drives this team you brought together. What would be the compelling outcome? Use the "to do what?", "so what?" line of questioning. This is the aspirational language that brings those you're working with together. Make it specific enough and aligned with the organization's goals. These conversations will provide the team with a sense of direction—an organizational compass.

3. Agree on the Operational Principles of the Team

    a. Together as a team, create the norms for a climate of collaborative results. These are the operating principles, specific values, behaviors, and the type of environment where team members can do their best work. These norms are related to the specific work.

        »   What could get in the way of reaching the results?

        »   What does good work look like?

» What would the difference between stagnating and thriving look like?

4. Decide on the Critical Goals

   a. As a leader, have the conversation about *what are the critical goals for the year?* Consider what goals can be parsed out to other teams, as opposed to having them all remain with the leadership team. Carefully consider who needs to be on each team.

   b. What will success look like? How will the team measure whether the goals have been achieved? Which agreed-upon metric will be used to assess whether the goal has been successfully reached?

5. Clarify Procedures, Roles, and Responsibilities

   a. These are conversations which enable you to co-create with your team using the kind of clarity that moves projects forward. They allow everyone to become clear about who does what and how critical decisions are made.

   b. How will members hold each other accountable and what are the consequences for work not executed properly?

As a leader promoting a climate for collaborative results, remember *how* you say something—your tone of voice, and other nonverbal cues—is as important as *what* you say. As a leader, be mindful that your words are powerful and come across as if broadcasting with a megaphone. In a team meeting, a leader might say: "As we go around the table, I am going to ask all of you to share your thoughts about the proposed product. I will go last. I want to make sure each of you can voice the good, the bad, and the ugly, without being influenced by my perspective."

Put this simple conversational secret in place and many of the issues usually attributed to disruptive behaviors will magically disappear, especially during this time of uncertainty and volatility.

As you spoke with caring and candor, people started to be more open in voicing important points of view. People began to own up to mistakes and ask for help before things became big issues. People stopped hoarding information to protect themselves from being blamed. Team members started to trust you, as the blame game had ceased and practicing a feed-forward ethos created a positive climate.

You became open to changing your mind. You listened and stopped interrupting people. People expressed that they now knew you had always cared about them, you just never showed it before. The result? Despite the difficulties of the pandemic and being remote, the virtual team pulled together and were more productive than before. The leadership team members shared that they too thought they became better leaders for their own teams. They slowly walked the walk in their own teams and began to teach their own teams how to apply these conversation secrets.

DOWN THE LINE: WHAT HAPPENED TO OUR COURAGEOUS LEADER?

It's now almost a year later. You have applied and practiced these conversation secrets to generate trust, connection, and collaboration. Sometimes you surprised yourself and were successful. Sometimes you were hesitant to try using one of them and then regretted that. And at times, despite your best intentions, one of the conversational tools didn't work the way you had intended. This is to be expected. The more you practice, the more the conversational secret tools become second nature to the way you talk and create a culture of collaboration, connection, and trust.

You think enough time has passed now to assess the impact of the new ways of having conversations. You engage external consultants to interview your leadership team members to find out the impact of applying the conversation tools. You then have consultants interview members of your leadership's own teams. You also ask the consultants to examine the larger impact from other stakeholder perspectives. You include interviews with the customers and the community leaders that your employees routinely have conversations with at regular intervals. What worked well? What didn't? What changes happened? What, if any, were the tangible and intangible results? You are glad that the interviews were confidential, so that members could speak freely.

The key findings surprise you. The comments are clear. Leadership team members identify that you, their leader is the one who has changed the most. Your eyes crinkle, and the corners of your mouth form a smile, as you whisper under your breath, so people *have* noticed a positive change. The report indicates that people felt a change in the nature of the conversations which positively impacted the engagement in meetings and altered the culture within the team for the better. People stopped hoarding information to protect themselves from being blamed. Team members started to trust you, as the blame game ceased and practicing a feedforward ethos created a positive climate.

People indicate they welcome your delegating more and how you became open to changing your mind when someone presented a compelling case. You listen more carefully and empathetically now, and that has had an impact on people being able to connect with you. People expressed that they now know you had always cared about them, you just never showed it before.

The result? Despite the difficulties of the pandemic and being remote, the virtual team pulled together and were more productive than before.

The leadership team members shared that they too thought they became better leaders for their own teams. They slowly walked the walk in their own teams and began to teach their own teams how to apply these conversation secrets.

The journey of personal awareness and transformation has been tough on you. You have had to change the way you have been taught as the right way to lead. Yet reading this report makes it all worth it. This candor, caring and openness is meaningful to people. You never realized, as a leader, how much they needed you to be human too. As you read these comments you try hard not to show the emotion swelling inside you. You had always been a tough and fair leader, and that had been fine with you. Now you begin to recognize just how meaningful these results are to you as an individual, not just as a leader, and the feedback has touched you deeply.

There *is* an alternative way to lead that is more powerful and effective than just leading through authority, with only shareholder results in mind. You realize how much you have grown in this leadership crucible through the pandemic. You finally realize that it is your own empathy, trust, and connection with people that has empowered people and their teams. People have noticed and have responded by bringing their hearts and hands to work. They care about you too, you reflect quietly. You continue in silent reflection, how it has taken the pandemic of 2020 to wake you up to recognize that the key to successful leadership is truly having empathy for and taking care of the people you work with—to be of and for the people.

The report indicates that leadership team members also experience themselves as more effective leaders, as have their own teams. The impact, people have said, comes from changing the nature of conversations which changes the climate in the teams and positively impacts engagement in the workplace. The leader sets the example. The leadership teams set the example and people begin to realize, the change is here to stay.

You are curious as to whether customers had noticed the difference in conversations. The results from the customer data blew you away. This is more than just a trickle-down effect; this is a culture transformed. The customers took the time to comment how appreciative they are of the care and conversations your employees are now having with them. You chuckled, when you read in the report, that customers wanted to know what training you have given people that they listened so well. They want that for their teams too.

When the consultants interviewed community stakeholders where the company is located, the responses were similar. The community has always appreciated the company for being socially responsive and having donated money to community causes. What they celebrate now is how the "check and a photo op" has evolved. It now includes quality conversations with senior representatives on how to contribute beyond money, to create much needed change in the community.

You are pleased that the consultants have shared with you that if you stay this course you can expect employee engagement scores to continue to increase. This is good news. You are aware that every percent increase in engagement translates to bottom line results—for all stakeholders. Your face softens. Now you understand how organizations with leaders who inspire trust and have cultures of connection and collaboration are more likely to have higher engagement. You realize that it also means a fuller engagement—a culture in which people work with both hearts and minds.

Retention too, is much higher, the consultants suggest, as people want to remain in this type of a work environment. Retention also helps the bottom line as it costs a year's salary to train someone new in your organization. Of course, people want to remain at work in this type of environment. You know how important it is to tomorrow's leaders, and to millennials, that they receive feedforward often. They need to know they're valued and appreciated. You reflect for a moment to yourself, and don't all people have the drive to be recognized and have their voice heard?

You share with your team that the secret power of conversations can be found in neuroscience. We now understand more about the neuroplasticity of the brain. The phrase "Neurons that fire together, wire together" was first used by Donald Hebb, a Canadian neuropsychologist—meaning our brain can keep on wiring new neurons so we can continue to learn throughout our lives. For example, conversations of synergy unleash the electric energy we all have in our somatic systems, in our bodies.

Neurochemicals like the oxytocin, the feel-good bonding chemical of love, gets released when we trust someone, when we connect in relationships, when we enjoy collaborations at work. You smile to yourself. Yes, there is some elemental neuroscience at the heart of these conversation secrets. What you do know clearly now is that these conversations have the power to transmit positive forces which in turn transform individuals, teams, and organizations through creating trust, connection, and collaboration.

Improved engagement and retention scores are good to have. The real key for you is that both your leadership team members, and others who have been interviewed express enjoying their work, despite all the pressures from the outside. People feel they can have the hard conversations in ways they can understand others, and have people hear them. They also express pride that the company is beyond maximizing shareholder profit, and that having all stakeholders in mind is meaningful to more than the millennial population. These last comments bring another reflection to mind.

It took this pandemic to make you realize the severity of unequal impact on humanity. You "woke-up" from your denial and decided to be proactive and transition the company to a stakeholder-centric business model, which is at the heart of Stakeholder Capitalism. You did it because it is the right thing to do. What you didn't realize was how powerfully inspiring this had become for your leadership team members.

You are pleased to share the results of the consultant's report with the leadership team and how research suggests that 80% of results can be traced back to the leaders. The team is visibly moved by the results of the report that team engagement, retention and productivity have improved, and the powerful bottom line impact of the conversations of leaders. What you didn't expect is that the team would decide to embed these conversation secrets so quickly into the rest of the organization. You partially covered your mouth with your hand because you didn't want to take the chance the team would see you muffle the sounds of quiet laughter.

You had to hold yourself back from reminding the leadership team how resistant they were initially when you proposed the idea of using the conversation secrets to change the way conversations are usually held at the company. You had to quickly remind yourself of the conversation tools, and zip your mouth shut. You tell yourself to cherish the moment. Your leadership team has become the champion of the conversation secrets. You slowly take your hand away from your mouth. You let the team know how proud you are of their decision. You can let go of the need to control everything and let them shine. You notice how much more self-reflection you are doing lately, rather than responding impulsively and charging ahead. This experience is transforming you and your team. You eagerly look forward to the time when the conversation secrets will be embedded throughout the entire organization.

Your story doesn't end here. Your company's reputation has grown, and you have been quietly tapped on the shoulder to merge with a much larger company. You think to yourself, "Thank goodness we now have the conversation secrets on our side."

And that, my friends, is for another story.

EPILOGUE

The focus of *Conversation Secrets* *for Tomorrow's Leaders* was initially intended for executives in the corporate world. The more we wrote, the more we recognized that leaders are everywhere—at work, in the community, and in our own families. These everyday leaders can all benefit from learning these conversation secrets which build trust, connection, and collaboration.

We are confident there is a path forward in this ever-changing world—if we move with a growth mindset and with open hearts. And since all change begins with listening and with conversations, that is how you as the leader can have significant impact. A recent Gallup poll states that 69% of people don't trust their politicians, 57% don't trust business leaders, and more than half don't trust the media. Leaders who practice and introduce these 21 conversation secrets can have a great impact on mitigating these results.

The world-wide awakening or paradigm shift has accelerated the change in the future of work, where people work and how employees and all stakeholders are to be treated and to share in the abundance. The importance of leaders showing empathy and caring for the work life integration of employees is gaining momentum. Emotion and vulnerability long banned from the workplace, is being normalized.

Our TV weather forecaster was broadcasting from his home, and his two young daughters caught him off guard as they came on the set and sweetly upstaged him. Embarrassed, he turned a shade of red, showed his vulnerability to the audience and continued with the weather. The audience ratings went wild for the adorable girls. We all resonate with his predicament. We understand the duality of work and life during the pandemic in a way we have refused to acknowledge before. As a leader, maximizing profits is only one measure of success. The ability to have empathy, to create trust and relationships and a culture of collaboration, innovation and quickly adapt are the new normal of success to thrive as future fit leaders.

We invite you to apply the 21 conversation secrets, and strengthen the trust, connection, and collaboration as the foundation of a culture of innovation necessary to succeed in the future. So, take the risk, experiment with these 21 conversation secrets. Be the role model and walk the talk. The people you lead will learn by watching how you lead during these difficult times.

Now that you've finished reading our book, we are confident you have found some golden nuggets to apply for greater impact in your leadership journey. Or perhaps something else brought you to this page. Either way, you have decided to invest in your leadership capability for positive change—and this is worth celebrating. We trust that when you start experimenting with one or more of the 21 conversation secrets, you will notice a positive impact. We ask that you pay it forward by sharing one or more of the 21 conversation secrets with people you know—your team members, leaders, colleagues, and friends. Whether you are president of a company or of a country, whether you are a celebrity, a mom, or a community activist, you have the same capacity to change your conversations and change the world, one conversation at a time.

REFERENCES

1   "Build trust by understanding the rules of engagement", HR Zone, accessed 19 December 2020, https://www.hrzone.com/engage/employees/build-trust-by-understanding-the-rules-of-engagement.

2   Judith E. Glaser, *Conversational Intelligence: How Great Leaders Build Trust and Get Extraordinary Results* (Brookline: Bibliomotion, 2014).

3   Bill McFarlan, *Drop The Pink Elephant: 15 Ways to Say What You Mean... and Mean What You Say* (Oxford, UK: Capstone Publishing Ltd, 2004).

4   Karen Kimsey-House et al., *Co-active Coaching* (4th ed.) (London: Nicholas Brealey Publishing, 2018).

5   Douglas Stone et al., *Difficult Conversations: How to Discuss What Matters, Most* (New York: Penguin Books, 2010).

6   Mark Goulston, *Talking to "Crazy": How to Deal with the Irrational & Impossible People in Your Life* (New York, NY: HarperCollins Leadership, an imprint of HarperCollins, 2016).

7   Srinivasan Pillay MD, *Life Unlocked:7 Revolutionary Lessons to Overcome Fear* (New York, NY: Rodale Books, 2010).

8   David Rock, *Quiet Leadership: Six Steps to Transforming Performance at Work* (New York, NY: HarperCollins Publishers, 2007).

9   Judith E. Glaser, "Your Brain Is Hooked on Being Right", Harvard Business Review (28 Feb 2010).

10   "Feedforward" is a term coined by Marshall Goldsmith in his book, *What Got You Here Won't Get You There: How Successful People Become Even More Successful* (Mark Reiter Hachette Books, 2007).

11   Wikipedia contributors, "Framing effect (psychology)," *Wikipedia, The Free Encyclopedia*, https://en.wikipedia.org/w/index.php?title=Framing_effect_(psychology)&oldid=999607353 (accessed February 1, 2021).

12   Bernard Mayer, *The Dynamics of Conflict Resolutions: A Practitioner's Guide* (San Francisco, Jossey-Bass, 2000), 132.

13   Gloria Feldt, *No Excuses: Nine Ways Women Can Change How We Think About Power* (New York: Seal Press, 2012).

14   "There were no weapons of mass destruction in Iraq", The Guardian, accessed June 1, 2020, https://www.theguardian.com/world/2004/oct/07/usa.iraq.

15   Simon Sinek, *The Infinite Game* (Portfolio/Penguin: 2019) p. 120.

16   Daniel Goleman, "Leadership That Gets Results", *Harvard Business Review*, (March-April 2000).

17   Virginia Tower Burden, *The Process of Intuition* (Theosophical Publishing House: 1975).

18   Andreas Weber, *Enlivenment: Towards a Fundamental Shift in the Concepts Nature, Culture, and Politics* An Essay, Volume 31 of the Publication Series Ecology (Published by the Heinrich Böll Foundation Berlin 2013)

19   Daniel Christian Wahl *Designing Regenerative Cultures* (Triarchy Press, Axminster England: 2016)

ABOUT THE AUTHORS

Dr. Mindy L. Gewirtz mgewirtz@collaborativenetworks.net

Mindy is a Leadership, Career and Team Coach for the C-Suite and tomorrow's leaders. Clients develop a growth mindset accelerating trust, connection, and collaboration to achieve exponential results. Mindy is master level certified coach (MCC) and Adjunct Faculty at Lewis University in the master's program on Organizational Leadership. She's also faculty and mentor coach for Potential Genesis HR in India. Her global client companies span high-tech, biotech, cleantech, financial services, and government. Mindy is a speaker and co-author of five book chapters on leadership, teaming and change.

Steve Hamilton-Clark *steveclark232@gmail.com*

Steve has the unique combination of CEO experience and Executive Leadership & Mentor Coach expertise. He focuses on developing future fit leaders through his global coaching practice The 18th Camel Ltd. and, as a Partner & Head of Faculty, trains Leaders as Coach through The Henka Institute, an International Coach Federation accredited program. Steve is a Canadian and British citizen born in Dubai, fluent in French, and educated around the world.

Carrie E. Gallant *carrie@gallantsolutionsinc.com*

Carrie Gallant is a dynamic speaker, executive leadership coach and negotiation strategist, formerly an executive, practicing lawyer and adjunct law professor at the University of British Columbia. Carrie weaves psychology, neuroscience, and improvisation with strategy as she inspires and empowers her clients to think bigger, negotiate more powerfully and step up into greater influence and impact. She is the founder of The Gallant Leader™ Institute, a Negotiation Consultant with ENS International and certified in Conversational Intelligence® and Authentic Leadership for Teams®.

For more information and resources please visit us at http://www.21ConversationSecrets.com or contact any one of us by email.